Dr. William Alfred McCartney, ThD., C.M.G.

ISBN: 9798874493462

DEDICATION

Dr. William Alfred McCartney, ThD. C.M.G.
February 7th, 1926 - August 5th, 2021

This book was written by Dr. William 'Al' McCartney. This is a story of the McCartney and Allen families of Tarpum Bay, Eleuthera. It tells of perseverance and of success in entrepreneurship, while walking by faith. This story takes us through the journey of Dr. William Alfred McCartney and his dedication to God and Family. His memories will resonate throughout generations as a part of his legacy.

The memories in this book are the recollection of Dr. William 'Al' McCartney, and are told in his own words.

"When pursuing your goals, always have faith."
- Dr. William Alfred McCartney, ThD., C.M.G.

'The Journey of a 20th Century Eleutherian'

Autobiography of Dr. William 'Al' McCartney

TABLE OF CONTENTS

Preface

Honourable Perry Gladstone Christie, P.C.
Former Prime Minister of The Bahamas

Al McCartney's book, "The Life of Al" is an invaluable tool for ordinary people, not just in The Bahamas, but the world. For those who seek inspiration and a model of integrity, hard work, creativity and generosity in business and in life.

Al, posthumously through this work; defines for us the purposeful life and the spirit of humility and kindness, with a homespun ethic, stern values, and carefully chosen directions drawn from his Christian faith.

I am fortunate to have been asked to write this foreword for this book penned by such an extraordinary man and published in extraordinary times which require extraordinary faith, discipline, courage, integrity and human decency.

Here we are in the throes of the deadliest pandemic faced by three generations, yet Al McCartney is able to show us in this wonderful book that struggle, disappointment, the crush of life, and the frustration ambition can weave; are all surmountable. There is no time for blame, self-defeat and jealousy, or lack of self-esteem. Like Al, 'you just simply get on with it.'

This story is also the history of the McCartney and Allen families of Tarpum Bay, Eleuthera. Al McCartney finishes his formal education at the age of 13. He then arrives to Nassau the capital, where so many just like him had come before, only to be bruised and scattered in the big city. He has come from an island farming community of tomatoes and fishing; but the lessons learned have readied him for his season.

He becomes a Christian at the age of 24 and his walk with faith in the Brethren Church Ministry is now legendary. Al entered the greasy, back breaking, heavy lifting world of auto body mechanics, where his honesty grew his business. He achieved two major car dealerships for high-end European brands; all the while he continued to mentor and train a new cadre of auto body mechanics for their personal ventures.

This story shall be read and enjoyed by generations unborn. It is not a "rags to riches" story. It is a story about standing on the promises of what Al accepted and believed when he chose to become a believer, a worker, and a leader in his church.

For those of us who believe in the family unit, Al presents a recipe for a successful union, fathering; and not just his own, but mentoring in the church and the wider community. His wife Eileen was his faithful and enduring partner, friend, critic, and lover.

Al McCartney's testimony in this book is a workable blueprint for success for all who dare follow in his footsteps. Al shows and demonstrates how it can be done. There can be no more excuses. This is a book every parent would want to read to their children, and a must have in every family bookcase. A referenced work for every professional and aspiring nation builder.

Enjoy!

Honourable Perry Gladstone Christie, P.C.
Former Prime Minister of The Bahamas

Al with his mother, Addie Dell

Tribute to Al McCartney

Dr. David Allen

Al McCartney lived an exemplary life which earned him the right to be called a National Bahamian Hero. Al McCartney was a Christian leader in family life, the church, and all parts of our community. He possessed a powerful and hopeful vision for his beloved country, The Bahamas. As my cousin, I sought his consultation on numerous occasions, and he was always available to meet and listen to me. I led The Bahamas National Task Force on drugs during the National Cocaine Epidemic in the 1980s. This was a tremendous challenge and exposed me to some of the most painful, daunting, and impossible situations. Often, I was discouraged, but Al in his cheery way would always smile and say, "don't give up." After writing a series of scientific articles to describe the Cocaine Crisis in The Bahamas, I felt the time had arrived for me to tackle the social fragmentation resulting from the cocaine epidemic. I decided to start a community group therapy project which would encompass the prison, the reform schools, orphanages, and all the marginalized areas ravaged by The Cocaine Epidemic.

In 2006, I started a group with seven mothers, all who had a son murdered within the country. First it was hard for them to trust me, and I had to earn my right to visit them in their community. Within a year, the group expanded to over thirty people, including drug addicts and people that were victims of violent crimes. As the group grew, I noticed the church where we were having the meetings became more distant and one Wednesday afternoon when I showed up with my group, the church guard said he was not given authority to open the room. He implied that the people were worried about the kinds of persons I was bringing around the church. My heart sank and as I looked at my people, I said, "we were not going to give up." I told them I believed that God would provide a place on East Street to meet at this time next week.

Contacting Al McCartney, I told him of my pain, and felt that I had to find a place to meet because the program was growing, and the spirit of God was beginning to work in a powerful way. The end result was the following: Al McCartney arranged for us to meet at the East Street Gospel Chapel. This became the most strategic and largest of The Family People Helping People Project. The group grew between fifty and sixty persons. It consisted of people convicted of murder, persons suffering from domestic abuse, violent crimes, mental illness, and persons referred by the courts. The meetings would start at 4pm and go until about 6pm. This meant that some nights during the winter months, when I came out of a meeting, it was actually dark. One night, to my surprise, sitting outside in his parked car was Al McCartney. I went over to him and asked him, "What are you doing?" He said, "I just came to pray for you all. Our country needs this. We can't let this work die." Even though he received a lot of opposition from within, he persevered with us. Inmates on parole, victims of violence, drug addicts, and others from all walks of life were blessed and came to receive hope and a new way of life.

In March 2020, we had to discontinue the meetings in person and continue meeting by Zoom due to Covid-19. Since then, until now, a number of people were murdered, sent to prison, gave up hope and attempted suicide, but we will return. Each week I get a call from parents and families asking when we will start again. The Family Helping People Project was chosen to represent new ways of dealing with real world problems at The Hochberg Lecture at the annual American Group Psychotherapy Conference in Houston Texas 2018.

Many persons have been blessed by the project, but the little-known factor is that we were only able to survive because Al McCartney fought for us. That is the nature of Al McCartney, a National Bahamian Hero. Please read this book and realize that you are not reading about a mere man, but about the visitation of a person embodied with a transcendent vision of hope and peace for our country.

Thank You.
Yours Respectfully,

David F. Allen M.D., M.P.H., O.D.
Distinguished Life Fellow of the American Psychiatric Association

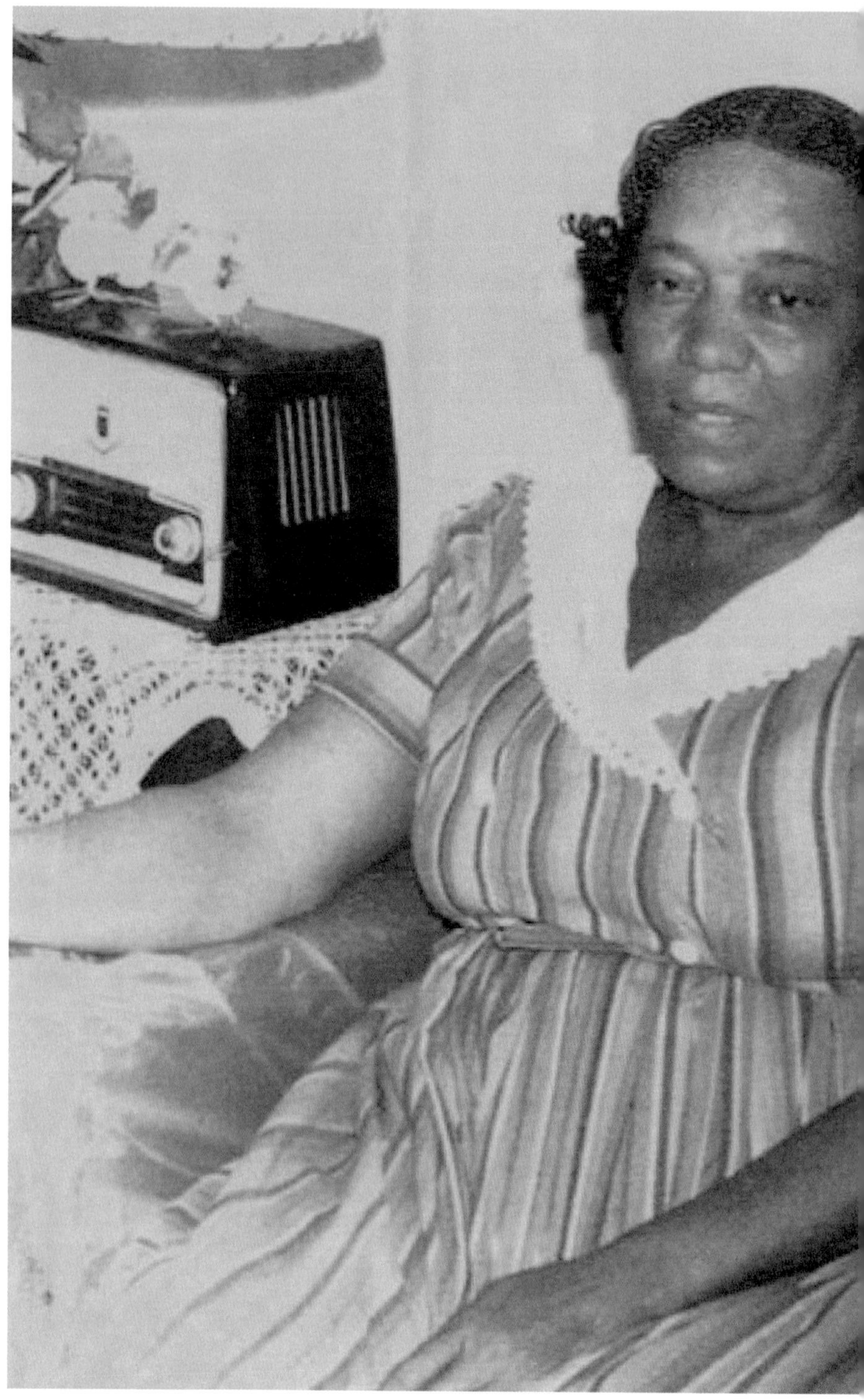

Al's Parents; Alfred Arnold & Addie Dell

1
In the Beginning

The Infant Baby Boy "Al"

I, William 'AL' Alfred McCartney Sr., first child of Alfred Arnold and Addie Dell McCartney, was born on February 7th, 1926 in Tarpum Bay, Eleuthera, The Bahamas. My mother, Addie Dell (Allen) McCartney, was affectionately called 'Mama'.

Our home was located on the corner of Lord and Victor Streets. It was a quaint house with four rooms, a high roof, and an attic. It had an outside toilet and a kitchen away from the home. In those days our home was considered to be very stylish.

McCartney Family Tarpum Bay Homestead

My father purchased a baby carriage that had large wheels and very good suspension. It was made of wicker and had a top that moved back and forth. I described my baby carriage because it came in very handy for me around age eleven or twelve.

Tarpum Bay, in my humble opinion was the best laid out town in Eleuthera at that time. There was an eight mile stretch of sandy beach across the Bay. The people were proud and very industrious. My three sisters were born within the next five years.

Al's Immediate Family: Front row: (left to right) Brother-Arnold, Mother-Addie, Father-Alfred: Rear row: Al,Sisters: Ruth, Ivis, Dorothy & Angela.

Al with mother & siblings: Ivis, Ruth, Dorothy (Dot), Angela & Arnold

Al's Paternal grandfather: William Ashwer McCartney

My Grandfather's Kiss

A terrible hurricane hit The Bahamas in August 1926. My grandfather, William Ashwer McCartney, his son Charlie, as well as others were aboard their Schooner, 'The Imperial', when they were all swept away by a huge wave and lost at sea. The 'Imperial' was a two masked vessel which was known to be very fast.

I was told that the morning before the hurricane struck, my grandfather, who lived not far away from us, stopped at our home on his way to where 'The Imperial' was anchored. He came to my crib and gave me a kiss. He then continued to 'The Imperial', pulled up the anchor, then tried to sail around the coast to Rock Sound which was known as a safe harbour.

Only a single mask from 'The Imperial' was ever found. Persons who witnessed the tragedy said that 'The Imperial' entered Rock Sound harbour but was swept away into the ocean by a gigantic wave. Documents indicated that William Ashwer McCartney was a brilliant, caring and industrious visionary. Since 1926 his memory still lives on through family, his unselfishness, and his holdings.

Incident with Ruth

"Thank God she wasn't hurt!" At age seven, I ran out to save my sister, Ruth, who was just four years old, from being run over by a truck driving up Lord Street!"

Al's Oldest sister, Ruth

At around 9 a.m., Ruth and l were playing in the front yard of our home. A truck that was driving east on Lord Street approached the McCartney's house when our younger sister Ruth ran out of the yard into the trucks path. Fortunately, the driver spotted her and applied brakes. Ruth, still not paying attention, fell. The driver was able to stop in time. When l saw what was happening, I was able to pick her up. She had no injuries, but was frightened and crying. She surely was more careful after that matter! I then cleaned off Ruth's legs, and we both went back into the house and locked the door. Mama was upset because the play place and kitchen were on opposite sides of the house. It was a good experience to prepare us for our move to Nassau.

Relocating to Nassau

In 1933, I was seven years old and for economic reasons my father decided to relocate our family, the four siblings (Al, Ruth, Ivis, and Dorothy), to Nassau.

He traveled ahead to Nassau to find housing for our family. I remember getting into the dingy boat and being "sculled" out to the M.V. Priscilla. I was lifted on board and put into a room with two bunk beds. Off to Nassau we sailed. We were met by our father at Prince George Wharf who placed us into a horse and carriage (surrey), and took us to a house through a corner just opposite the gate of the police barracks. It seemed like we were under a huge water tower. We occupied two rooms of a house, while a lady tenant occupied the other section. The lady tenant's name was Miss Minette and her son's name was Austin. The Charltons lived opposite our house. Our house was barricaded with boards across the back door. One day Dorothy leaned too far over and fell onto the honey-combed rocks.

Water Tower, Nassau, The Bahamas

We lived there for a while getting familiar with the surroundings. We made many friends and my parents began to seek out a school for us to attend. Mortimer's Candy Kitchen was not far away. I remembered vividly Amos Mortimer, one of the chief candy makers, who would throw the scraps of candy in the back disposal bin after the candy was shaped and wrapped. We little boys would sit on the back steps awaiting Amos' arrival with the candy scraps for ourselves.

I also remember the Sands girl who lived next door. She was our first visitor, and she took me to Kirk School at the Presbyterian Church. This was a pleasant experience. Summertime they held an August picnic on 'Hog Island' now Paradise Island. This began a lifelong connection with the Sands family. I learned later that the Sands family was closely related to the Sands family of Savannah Sound.

After six months our family was relocated to a two bedroom house which had no kitchen or bathroom. It was one block east of East Street on the southern side of Mason's Addition. After school there was lots of cricket playing on that street.

Sometimes the ball would get lost in weeds under the floor of the house. A group would then rush over to me shouting "hey island boy, where is the ball?" Frightened, I would reply, "I ain't gat de ball. Doreen, (Doreen Dawkins, the girl next door), dey gat de ball."

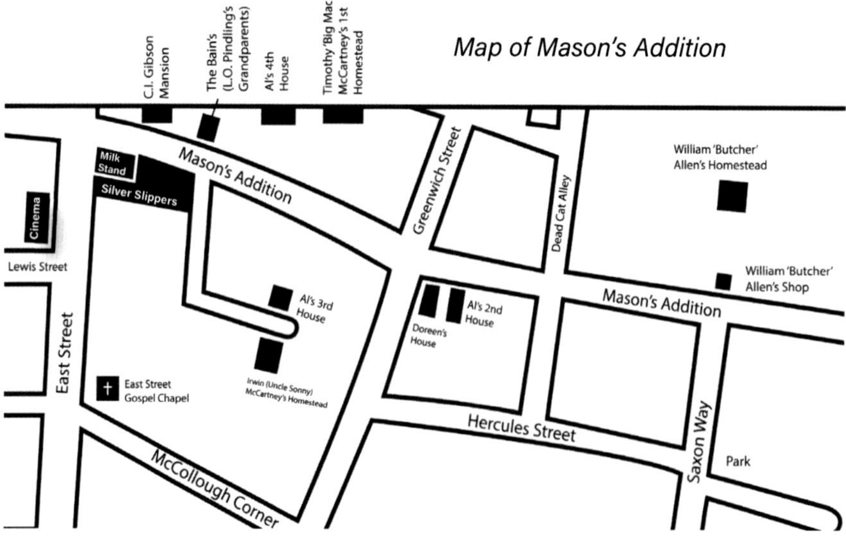

Nearly every time I met any of those boys they would mock me with that. A year later, the family moved again to a house opposite Uncle Sonny (Irwin McCartney) and Aunt Olga which I felt was good, as we were close relatives.

Maternal grandfather: William Wilkerson Allen ('Willie Butcher')

The Allens Move to Nassau

A few years later, Grandpa, William 'Butcher' Wilkerson Allen relocated to Nassau to east Mason's addition after the death of his wife Bayanna in 1936.

Uncle Fred, (Butcher Allen's eldest son) who was a farmer, moved his family to Nassau at the beginning of the tomato season to start a farm in the eastern part of the island. He moved one house above us on the top of the hill in the Mason's Addition area. I recall that the Jehovah Witnesses were just getting established in The Bahamas at the time. They had their loudspeakers in uncle Fred's yard on the precipice of the hill overlooking Mason's Addition, broadcasting all over the community. As children we did not know what it was all about, but we enjoyed the excitement none-the-less. Jehovah Witnesses are now established all over The Bahamas. Our families, Fred Allen and the McCartney's had Junkanoo groups and "rushed" in groups on the hill beating pots and pans for drums and blowing paper-made horns. The Junkanoo rush was attended by Aunt

"Bessie" (Uncle Fred's wife) and Doris Carey (Freda Carey's sister) who worked as a home keeper for many years. We had many disagreements. I remember one in particular where my cousin George Allen threw an old frying pan and cut my sister Ivis, on the head.

Sister: Ivis Beatrice

Grandpa, 'Butcher' Allen, had purchased property opposite the Father Cooper Park. He afforded all his children a lot each. My father rejected the offer while uncle Eris Allen accepted the offer and went to live on the property with Aunt Sylvia, and their children, Wayne, Clarke, and Julian.

Uncle Fred's family later moved to the corner of Shirley & Armstrong Streets. Alfred and Addie's family soon moved to the property at the end of McCartney Lane, which is on the southern side of Wulff Road, two blocks east of East Street. From all accounts, a good choice was made by all the families. Aunt Naomi Allen-Christie (Butcher Allen youngest daughter) went on to train in nursing and as a mid-wife. Aunt Bertha Allen-Ferguson worked as a seamstress with Eva Williams on Fredrick Street. That gave me an opportunity to pay Aunt Bertha a visit as I worked on Bay Street near the Straw Market. Aunt Bertha would 'spot' me at the door and she would give me two or three pennies that I used as snowball money. She went on later to marry George Ferguson, a taxi-cab driver.

Addie's sister: Nurse Naomi Allen-Christie

Uncle Bill Carey and his wife Aunt Ruth Allen-Carey also moved to Nassau and joined grandpa in Mason's Addition. This was the beginning of the "trio"- grandpa Butcher, Fred, and Bill. This "trio" developed over 100 acres of land with tomato farming. Grandpa was able to farm 100 acres on the east end of Nassau, the site that St. Andrew's School is now located on. The following year he farmed 100 acres on Soldier Road where Woodlawn Cemetery is now located. During the summer holidays on the farm I kept the men cool with well water when requested. Uncle Bill Carey suffered a stroke and thereafter worked as a bookkeeper for some time.

In grandpa's senior years, he went on to marry Miss Bertha Ferguson. I recall her being a "good natured" lady from Crooked Island. She came down with her father to work on my grandfather's farm. Grandpa spotted her and made an approach. Not long after they were standing before Brother Farrington to be married. Instead of working on the farm with Butcher, she became his wife and my step-grandmother for a long time after. Miss Bertha, as the grandchildren called her, was very kind. At most, I lost my position keeping grandpa's company. I was demoted, as he now had Miss Bertha.

2
Life in Nassau

Mason's Addition

My father then relocated the family to Mason's Addition. It was a two-room wooden home, located near the Silver Slipper night club, and the Cinema Hillside Theatre. The area was the 'Broadway' of The Bahamas on Saturday nights. It was called that because of the large numbers of persons that came out of those establishments at the same time on Saturday nights.

The young people would spend their time walking about shopping for ice cream cones from Rachel, all-day suckers from Mr. Royal, or checking out Mr. Johnson's property on East Street for one of the many Mameys (fruit) that fell from the popular tree.

Eastern Preparatory School No.1, ('Sands School') School Lane & Shirley Street

Between the ages of 8-10 years I attended Eastern Preparatory School, also known as Sands School, located on Shirley Street under the tutelage of Miss Sands, Agnes

Lightbourne and Mildred Hanna. We also attended the Central Gospel Hall Sunday school. Up to this time, we had no electricity or running water in our home. In the evenings, we would clean the lamp shades preparing them to be lit at night. By this time, for the first time in my life, I had my experiences with bed bugs. When the lamp was shut off you would feel the nipping from the bugs crawling out from the seams of the wood.

My standing job with Mrs. Gibson was that every morning before I left for school, I would deliver two buckets of water from the government water faucet below the hill. My pay was that every Saturday after baking I was given two pennies and a loaf of hot bread. The connection with the Gibsons was a lasting one. When I attended Western Junior High School, C.W. Sawyer was head teacher. After I graduated from there I attended Western Senior School, where C.I. Gibson was head teacher. Other teachers were Margaret Demeritte-McDonald, H.O. Nash, T.A. Thompson, Timothy Gibson, Kenneth Huyler, Miriam Cash-Dean and E.P. Roberts who was the teacher for woodwork. Unfortunately, my regret was leaving school at 13 ½ years without any certificates.

Just before my final weeks in school, my father was able to land me an apprentice position in the Tailor shop with Cecil Bethel tailoring. Most people had no electricity or running water in their houses. Very few had radios and some people had ice boxes. Milo Butler's truck would come around and you would purchase a six pence piece of ice and place it on the top of the box. It would last long enough to perhaps make some jello.

For fresh eggs, we would select the fat hens from your own chicken coop to lay, and for a good meal you would cut the head off the chicken, dip the body into hot boiling water, and pick all the feathers off to clean it and cook it. Soon there were small buildings scattered all over New Providence owned by

The Hatchet Bay Company where you could buy fresh chicken, fresh milk or a bottle of cracked eggs on Sunday mornings.

During this time, police arrests were very interesting. For example, when a person is arrested by the police in Mason's Addition he would be led by the hand of the police and walked to Central Station to be charged. Sometimes, the witness would follow the police to the station. Central Police Station was the nearest station to the "over the hill" community.

3
Mason's Addition

Well Known Families

Many well-known Bahamian families have roots in Mason's Addition. Many of our educators and civil servants were 'raised' there. Their upbringing began on East Street and Mason's Addition specifically. In Mason's Addition on the north side lived the Bains, Sir Lynden Pindling's grandparents. Sir Lynden spent a lot of time there. On the south side lived G.H. Thompson, grandparents of Michael "Sweet Bells" Thompson. Continuing east was a shop and then there was Doris Sands-Johnson, the Lockharts (who were grandparents of Calvin Lockhart, the movie star), Bertram Cooper member of East Street Gospel Hall Sunday School, and G.H. Thompson who was a family island teacher who sent his only son, Dewitt, to attend the Government High School. Their house was built four feet off the ground. I was sitting under the floor of the house when the older sister, Mable, was listening to the radio to hear her exam results. A loud applause went up.

Continuing east on the north side lived Sargent-Major Taylor. Up the hill were the Careys, Bill and Ruth (Parents of Dr. Baldwin, Faye Carey-Smith, Allan, Crystal, and Linda Carey-Jarrett). Further east on the south side was Carlton Francis' parents' home and north of that was Donald W. Davis (where he held evening classes). Next to him was W.W.

'Butcher' Allen (my grandfather). Next to him was the O'Briens whose son was High Commissioner to England and a cabinet officer.

The corner south of Mason's Addition off East Street is McCollough Corner where Leslie Miller's family lived. Located on west McCollough corner were the homesteads of Bishop Drexell Gomez's family, Mrs. Margaret Demeritte-McDonald, and the Hannas (Olive, Mazie, Caroline and their older sister who married a Greek businessman).

Living in Uncle Timmy's House on Mason's Addition Hill

We moved to two more locations before settling in Uncle Tim's house (mid-hill) on the north side of Mason's Addition. He had to relocate to Bethel's Addition or Glinton Square (now McPherson Street). The conditions on the hill was affecting his wife Aunt Cora's health. She would miscarry with every pregnancy while living on Mason's Additions' hill. After she was relocated to Glinton Square, she bore Timothy, Richard, Coramae, William (Wilmac), Joan, Mavis, Clinton, and Ann.

Now at the age of 10 years old I spent time at Eastern Prep then Western Junior where Cecil Bethel tutored. Other notorious people who attended were Sir Lynden Pindling, C.I. Gibson, Randal Fawkes, Thelma Gibson, Donald Davis, Doris Sands, G.H. Thompson and Carlton Francis. They all lived in Mason's Addition and witnessed over-the-hill "Broadway" in action.

Uncle Timothy's house was very accommodating. It was perched mid Fort Fincastle hill. It had a semi-circle porch. The view was breath-taking. We were able to see the tree-tops and, house-tops, so much so that during the winter looking south it appeared like a sea of snow because of a thick layer of mist. People were always passing by up and down the rocky alley slipping over the roots. Later the Government made steps to climb up and down.

A large tamarind tree in the south east corner of the yard always bore tamarinds. Although sour, it made a great past time for recreational activity. The house stood on stilts so that persons could walk upright when inside the home. There was a water pump, and I understand that being mid hill, it would sometimes lose it's 'prime' (pressure). The four-seat outside restroom was modern, although it had no running water. We played many games under the house floor. We made home movies using telephone cords and milk can receivers. The urine and 'stool' pots had to be kept under our beds until morning when they had to be emptied and cleaned.

I fully enjoyed that house and the lay-out as it was perched mid hill. To exit to the north one had to climb a bit higher past Mrs. Knowles and Mr. Cartwright's houses to a short path and onto a road which led to Mr. M. Sweeting and Mr. Fawkes' homes, then onto a park which then led to the Queen's Staircase (a.k.a '66 steps) and Fort Fincastle and The Water Tower.

Fort Fincastle (located on the 'Fort Hill')

The '66 steps' took us down to the out-patient department of The Bahamas General Hospital. Later the name was changed to Princess Margaret Hospital after The Princess's visit to The Bahamas. As young boys, games were always played under the streetlight which included (spinning) tops. Many times my top was split open by Randall Fawkes'. He would always "split" our small tops with his big tops.

Queen's Staircase (66 Steps), Nassau,Bahamas

Doctor Jackson Burnside's Dental Office was also located nearby. At the date of this writing August 28, 2017, I still have in my mouth a semi gold filling by Doctor Burnside from 1960, approximately 60 years ago.

Living at Uncle Tim's house afforded the opportunity to house some of our relatives who would come to Nassau for medical attention. I recall Aunt Bessie bringing Carlton and Darren for attention. Grandfather Butcher relocated to Nassau along with Aunt Bertha, and Aunt Naomi. They helped to sell off his products.

My relocation to Nassau gave me the opportunity to meet the family of C.l. Gibson. Both his and my family migrated from Eleuthera. The Gibsons were from Savannah Sound and my family was from Tarpum Bay. These settlements were just nine miles apart, yet there was a noticeable difference in dialect. At that time, Savannah Sound was known as the educational base of The Bahamas. Noted educators were born In Savannah Sound and lived there.

People like Timothy Gibson (the brother of C.I. Gibson) who became the author of our national anthem, 'March on Bahama Land' hailed from Savannah Sound. Many schools were also given the name of educators from Savannah Sound: C.I. Gibson, Charles W. Sawyer (son-in law of C.I. Gibson).

I became very friendly with Irwin, the youngest son of C.I. Gibson. I made it a practice to be present at meal-time when Mrs. Gibson would fix lunch for Irwin. Soon my father relocated us south of Wulff Road on his newly purchased property in Wilson Tract (now called McCartney Lane).

McCartney Lane Off Wulff Road

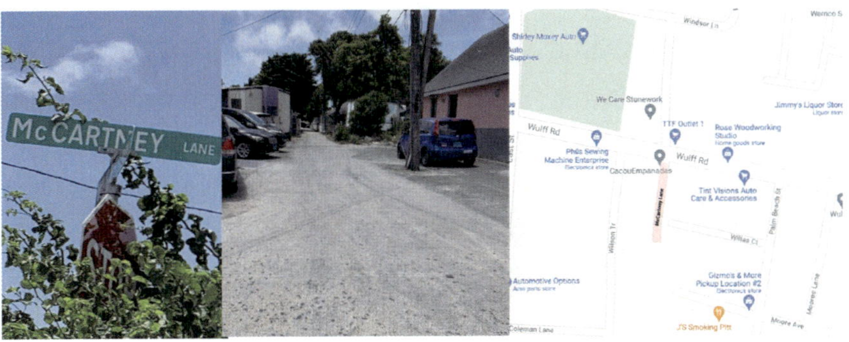

McCartney Lane, Nassau, The Bahamas

My family moved to McCartney Lane when I was eleven. The Road was 'honey-comb' rock, and we were without city water or electricity. The nearest faucet was three blocks away. Before going to school, I would load my five buckets into my baby carriage and push it from McCartney Lane to the corner of East Street and Wulff Road. After filling up the five buckets they were delivered to mama's kitchen for cooking and drinking purposes.

Sadly, my father was hospitalized for three weeks due to a nervous breakdown, little me had to walk down '66 steps' with lunch for him. I was not allowed to deliver the food because of my age. We hardly recognized him sitting on the veranda. I heard my father hallucinating. I cried because of fear of not knowing what would happen to my family. My family members were very kind to help us survive through this time.

My father, while alone at night would occupy himself by composing poems that was eventually published. One of his poems was 'The Sinking of the Imperial'. During his recuperation he did small jobs to help sustain the family including collecting sea shells & putting holes in them for jewelry manufacturing.

McCartney Lane Relocation

My father's small building in Tarpum Bay was dismantled and shipped to Nassau. It was trucked and stored on Grandpa 'Butcher' Allen's land in Mason's Addition opposite the park. After my father refused the land my grandfather offered him, he was fortunate to purchase land from Mrs. Higgs who owned some lots going south of Wulff Road just east of Windsor Park. The lot was 45x50 and had no utilities. It was the fifth lot in from Wulff Road, the eighth track on the rocky road. My father then removed the building material from grandpa's lot in Mason's Addition.

My father, still recovering from his illness begged his friend Bradfield Symonette from Rock Sound (the father of Nettica Symonette, owner of Cable Beach Hotel) to lay the foundation and put up the structure. The building was one story and took approximately six months to construct to the point where the family could occupy it. The restroom was an outside toilet with enough floor space to accommodate a metal wash tub. My father hired a man by the name of Willie Mingo to dig a well for our water supply. All ground water in that area was "brackish" so it could only be used for cleaning purposes.

I had a real outdoor experience. I used to build bird traps and the traps worked well. I raised and attended to chickens, goats, pigs and sheep. When I needed pig food from Mason's Addition I would go there on one foot of skate, pick it up in a gallon can, bring it back and feed my pigs. We would raise our animals and have them slaughtered but never ate any of the meat. The reason was that we felt like we were eating our own flesh. We preferred selling the animals and buying the equivalent.

Our kitchen had a kerosene two burner stove and an oven. My mother also possessed an oven made from a square wooden box lined with beaten metal from metal containers. Our washing was done by hand on a scrub board resting in the half wooden barrel tub that salt beef and pork were imported in. It was cut in half with handles on both ends. Washing water was made ready to use after it was soaked with ashes or charcoal. It was called 'lye' water. Our ironing was done with solid iron. The iron handle was detachable, and iron heated from lighted coal or a little long log burnt to charcoal. After the iron was heated it would be removed from the fire and rubbed on a rag to clean the smoothing surface and used to press clothes until it cooled. It was repeatedly placed on the fire to get hot. The next improvement was the 'goose' iron that was filled with charcoal, lit and allowed to burn to a glow. This provided a continuous hot iron until the coals burn out.

Kitchens were built separate and away from the dwelling. Most kitchens had ice boxes with a compartment on the top section to hold a solid piece of ice. The contents of the box were kept cool as long as the ice lasted. Most restrooms were outside the buildings built over a ditch with seats whereby you can sit and relieve yourself.

Our neighbours would visit & play games many evenings. A popular game was moonshine babies, where individual would lie on the patio floor and the outline of their body would be drawn with broken plate pieces. When the moon was bright the image stood out.

Our first electrical connection was through a sixpence meter. The rain water tank was the common water supply. All houses being built usually had one under the kitchen floor. Since moving to Wulff road my father was able to acquire quite a few acres of land. Most was acquired from the crown (four acres).

4
Joining the Workforce

William Alfred McCartney, Age 21

Tailoring Apprenticeship

During my summers and Saturdays my father was able to get an apprenticeship for me at Cecil Bethel's Tailoring. It was located next door to where my father worked. Mr. Hiram Newbold and Henry Lynch were also tailors at the shop. It was always an upscale tailor shop.

My assignment was to learn tailoring, work button holes, hem seams, and keep the goose-iron hot so that it would be ready when any tailor needed to use it. It was because of this job and the relationship I developed with Cecil Bethel that when he later became headmaster of The Government High School (G.H.S.), I was able to communicate with him about my son Barry transferring from St John's College. There were four other tailors at the shop. It is there that I met my lifelong friend, Willie-Mae Simms. Her brother, Rodrick, was also a tailor there. Later Willie Mae Simms married a Pratt and attended East Street Gospel Hall. She was able to contribute to the music of East Street Gospel Hall and years later began Little Learners Preschool at the church. The Willie Mae Pratt School for girls is named in her honor.

Another task I completed was running errands and purchasing items. At times I would be given three or four yards of material and on my way home, I would stop by Cecil Bethel's home to soak the material in a tub of water to shrink it. I would then hang the material on the clothesline and the next day it would be used to make pants or jackets.

The acquaintance with C.V. Bethel was also a link with my Central Gospel Chapel family. His brother Eddie's wife, Lilly, was from Central Gospel Chapel. She was the mother of Clement Bethel, Ruth Isaacs (the wife of Hon. Kendal Issacs), and Mark Irwin with whom I was acquainted. We were close friends until his death.

In the tailor shop there was a custom that never was explained to me. It was that every Christmas Eve night, all apprentices were given a dose of cod-liver oil and a soda before we left the shop. I never could understand the reasoning and did not pay it any attention. At the shop I met my future Aunt, Sylvia Allen who married my Uncle Eris Allen. She was the sister of Mrs. Pearl Cox of Augusta Street and grandmother of Sean McSweeney.

At lunch time, I would be present at the store on Bay Street. Sylvia liked to quiz me about my Uncle Eris, who at the time had recently graduated from Tuskegee College as one of the first qualified black electrical engineers in The Bahamas. She sent messages to Eris and I benefited by delivering and retrieving the messages as I was rewarded with ice cream, chocolates, and hot conch fritters. I made this a daily routine.

One of my fondest memories of Eris and Sylvia's courtship was when they invited me to attend a Cox, Clarke, and Allen family picnic in Adelaide. It's no surprise that I can remember vividly what we ate during that picnic. What stood out, as was it was my first time eating potato salad. It was a luxury and a real treat. After that I often asked mama to prepare this item at home. Needless to say, the relationship between Sylvia and Eris ended in marriage and three boys: Clarke, Wayne, and Julian.

5
Working on Cat Cay

Cat Cay, Luxury Island, The Bahamas

At 14, when I was finished school, I began to work with Uncle Eris for two years (until I was 17) as an electrical apprentice on Cat Cay. After approximately two years I returned to Nassau.

Uncle Eris Allen was a graduate of the prestigious black University, "The Tuskegee Institute". He became an electrical engineer and wired houses all over Nassau. I joined him because engineering was my interest. A major job that I can recall being involved with was at Zion Baptist Church. It had to be rebuilt because of major hurricane damage it sustained in the 1800's. I can vividly recall climbing high into the ceiling and installing connections while taking instructions from Rev. Talmage Sands, who later performed my marriage ceremony on June 27, 1951.

The only transportation Uncle Eris possessed was a bicycle. He sat me and the tools on the crossbar and rode east as far as McPherson bend to carry out his work.

Uncle Eris was awarded the appointment of manager of Electric Works and Power Station at the Cat Cay Resort. It was a private island with a hotel and casino - A deep sea, fishing resort in the Bimini Cays, 59 miles from Miami Florida. It was owned by Mr. Wacy of New York. There were yachts and private homes there. After he settled in, he sent for me knowing that this setup was just what I longed to be a part of. It had diesel engines, vehicles and yachts. When I received the invitation, my father said 'no way' he would allow me to leave home. I cried and I pleaded with my father and he gave me his final no. I then appealed to 'Grandpa Butcher Allen' who convinced my father to allow me to go. My grandfather told my father that, "the plan was for Eris to come back home after his studies in the U.S. to train the men of the family." My father gave me a four shilling note then asked Captain Milton Sweeting of the Tropical Trader to give me passage to Cat Cay.

I arrived at the dock at Cat Cay around 5 pm. The Cay was 1/2 mile wide and 2 1/4 miles long. I was met by Uncle Eris and we walked to our living quarters. It was about a 10 minute walk to a three story residence where the engineers resided. It was adjacent to the power station. My room windows faced east, and the engines were always running and very noisy. After I settled in, Aunt Sylvia served supper. At that time Clarkie was around three years old. I was still in short pants (boys were not allowed to wear long pants until they were 17 or 18 years old). Most of the employees resided in the eastern section of the Cay, while the executive staff resided in the center section of the Cay. If you wished for a restaurant or entertainment, you traveled to the native section about three quarters of a mile. I traveled to the restaurant for my favorite dish, bean soup and duff. I never forgot how it tasted. Sister Grant from Grand Bahama cooked the best bean soup I have ever tasted.

The first task my uncle had was to teach me how to drive. We used a little truck that had to be hand cranked. Every time I let my foot off the clutch too quickly the truck would stall, and Uncle Eris had to get out of the truck and crank it until the engine started. I stalled about three or four times until I became accustomed to easing off the clutch. This was just as Uncle Eris became angry. I learned to drive quickly, and soon I was on my own. No traffic, no police, and no street lights.

Soon I began wearing long pants and my legs and knees stayed a lot cleaner. I loved working in the power plant maintaining big engines. Some of which were eight feet high and a step ladder was needed to oil the top cylinder. Working around those heavy engines was my favorite task.

I wrote home frequently by surface mail, as quick communications was nonexistent. To send a telegram, the Cat Cay operator would send a Morse code message to Nassau that was typed by the receiver and then hand delivered. Unfortunately, six months after my arrival in Cat Cay, Aunt Sylvia became ill and Uncle Eris and his family moved back to Nassau. I decided to remain at Cat Cay under the tutorship of chief mechanic Delmar Vaughn, an American who was awaiting his call to service in the U.S. armed forces. I helped service and maintained the station for another year.

Since the war was still going on, no tourists visited, and no yachts ventured far from port because of the risk of being torpedoed by a German submarine. I was able to quickly learn from Delmar Vaughn a lot of engineering techniques, which later enabled me to qualify when applying for employment. We maintained fishing boats, yachts, golf carts and generators. My salary remained at two shillings per day and I proudly served and saved. Fortunately, I was not alone in the apartment building as Mr. & Mrs. Harry Sherman of Bimini were also residents. Harry was a fishing instructor.

Only radio communications from the U.S. mainland was available, so you had to depend on the talk shows for entertainment. There was no TV. Uncle Eris nor Aunt Sylvia returned to Cat Cay as she never regained her health. She bore two additional sons. I eventually returned to Nassau.

After the passing of Aunt Sylvia, Uncle Eris moved in with a lady by the name of Alice. He lived there until he became blind. He then moved in with his son Clarke where he lived until his death. Clarke was very helpful to my family as he grew older. Clarke died at the age of 70 and was survived by his wife Betty and children.

6
Business Begins

My Time After Cat Cay

After I arrived in Nassau from Cat Cay, the very next day I applied for employment as shift engineer at the Bahamas Electricity Corporation on Bay Street. Mr. Fred Moultrie offered me the position. At the same time, I also applied with the Americans who were building the Windsor Field and Oakes Field Airport. After three nights at B.E.C in 1946, I decided to accept the appointment of the posting from the Americans as an engineer. I was then hired by the U.S. post engineers to service power stations in Oakes Field and in Windsor field.

The Royal Air Force pilots were training there to fly. During the training many planes crashed all over New Providence especially on South Beach. In addition to serving standby equipment at power plants on Oakes Field as well as Windsor Field, I was also assigned to the plumbing section under the direction of Francis J. Smith of New York. He soon found that I could drive but had no driver's license. He took me to Central Police Station and requested them to grant me a license. I was issued a driver's license right away.

While working with the American Army post engineers, they quickly erected and maintained office buildings and barracks. They also taught the Royal Air Force (R.A.F.) men how to fly until the American Army Post engineers finished their assignment. After the Second World War ended, the post engineers left. The Bahamas government took control. I was then assigned to the Civil Aviation Department (C.A.D.) under the direction of Wing Commander E.H. Coleman, servicing operating equipment and transporting airplane fuel from Clifton Pier. Re-fueling the mess halls gave me an opportunity to receive monthly supplies of fried bacon and eggs served in empty peach cans. I made sure to refuel around breakfast time for that one reason. I continued to work at C.A.D. for a few more years.

In 1949, I felt the time was right to start my lifetime dream of owning my own garage. I informed Commander Coleman of my intention and told him that at the end of the following month I would resign. He indicated that he would refer C.A.D. jobs to me. I resigned and was given a garage license for McCartney Lane on March 31, 1949. I opened with a toolbox containing regular hand tools. I also built a ramp for lubricating cars and traveled to Miami to purchased a few pieces of equipment. My garage was promoted by 'word of mouth'. The intial sign read 'McAllen's Auto' because it was expected that it was to be a joint venture with my first cousin, George Allen, but George Allen and I went our separate ways. The business grew quickly. This was the birth of my extraordinary entrepreneurial skills which I perfected and which I pursued during my business legacy and church accomplishments. Commander Coleman kept his promise by giving me some Government repair jobs.

When I later got married in 1951, I relocated my business to Mt. Royal Ave. The business expanded even more. I was given business by the insurance companies and especially the taxi cab companies. This led me to increase my staff.

Later, I established a company in partnership with my father, Alfred Arnold McCartney and my brother, C. Arnold McCartney. The business was called McCartney (AAA) Triple "A" Automotive. We sold new, used, and rebuilt automotive parts and accessories.

In the 50's, McCartney's Auto Repairs was established for body and fender repairs and finishes. I trained many young men in the trade of auto body repairs. Many can attest to the endless hours worked by me and my staff. These apprentices, who nicknamed me "Deak" (abbreviation for deacon), included Everette Strachan, Delano Culmer, Tony Albury, Richard McCartney, John Bain, Joseph "Moose" Ferguson, Reginald Rigby, Rudy Pinder, and Sam Kemp. Hundreds of the nation's youth passed through my training. Some thought it was vigorous, but most were thankful in later years for the work ethic I instilled in them. In the early 1960's the Texaco Dealership was also granted, and a gas station was constructed.

In 1965, I established McCartney's Auto Company Ltd. that acquired the Fiat automotive dealership which was then held by Stanley V.S. Albury further North off Mount Royal Ave near Rosetta Street. It was dormant. Jack Shillan, (an Englishman who was a great customer and owned several Fiats and was also the developer of Palmdale), negotiated the dealership in New York. It was not realistic for a non-Caucasian to have gotten a franchise in those days.

While waiting for the Fiats to arrive at the vacant showroom, I became anxious. My brother in-law, L.B. Johnson and I moved forward to import and sell Moulton Bikes from England. These bikes were the first with shock absorbers, small wheels, and were able to fold in half so that you can store them easily in the trunk of a car.

The first Fiat order consisted of six cars – 1100 and 600 series models. Later the 850, 500 and 124 models were added. We also established a parts and service department for the Fiats. In 1967 I obtained a license to open a branch on Queen's Highway in Freeport, Grand Bahama next to Freeport Gas. Majority rule had just come in. Unfortunately, Pindling did not want to support my application as he felt that the Port Authority would have felt compelled to give it to me. I am grateful for the assistance that Mr. Garnett Levarity, (the then Government Administrator, (known as the chief). He was successful in obtaining the approval from the Port Authority.

Moulton Bike from England, ridden by Barry

First FIAT Dealership showroom with 3 of 6 of the first cars

A steel structure was then created to have a sales showroom and service departments. Ten cars were purchased and sent to Freeport and when we needed cars in Nassau, they were transported to Nassau by barge. The advantage was that import duty did not have to be paid until they left the Freeport zone. Eugene Edwards (ex-police officer from Trinidad), was the first sales manager in Nassau and was sent to Freeport, along with two Jamaican mechanics from our store, to operate that branch.

By 1968, the dealership had become financially burdensome and was sold to A.B.C. Motors. One of the conditions of the sale was that I work as the Service Manager of the company. There was also an exit clause. I resigned as Service Manager after one year.

Meanwhile, I partnered with my brother C. Arnold, Eugene Munroe, and Jim Martin to acquire the distributorship of the Dunlop Rubber Company to hold and operate this franchise.

Left Image: *Award for Texaco Dealer of the Month (photo with Bob Petit from Texaco local office).* ***Centre Image:*** *Tyre & Auto Suppliers: Being awarded Dunlop Tyre Distributorship. Photo with business partner , Arnold (brother), Dunlop Rep. from Jacksonville, William (Bill) Longsworth, manager.* ***Right Image:*** *FIAT convertible owned by Mr. Jack Shillan.*

The company Tyre & Auto Suppliers Ltd was established for this purpose. The company was owned by myself, my brother Arnold, and Eugene Munroe, as the Bahamian majority shareholders and minority shareholder Jim Martin Tyre Company of Jacksonville, Florida.

After a few years, Arnold and I bought out the shares held by Eugene Munroe and Jim Martin Tyre Co. This company expansion made it the largest supplier of automobile and heavy equipment tires in The Bahamas. The company was the distributor for Dunlop and Remington Tyres and accessories. Later, India Tyres, Sikkens, and Acme Paints were added in 1971. Tyre & Auto Supplies Limited acquired the Mazda franchise which was later sold to General Bahamian Company in 1983 (it was the parent company of A.B.C. Motors).

New Auto dealership showroom on Mt. Royal Ave

Simultaneously Commonwealth Textiles Limited was established. A Partnership with C. Arnold McCartney and Oscar Prioleau (Arnold's wife's brother-in-law). Four outlets were eventually opened in New Providence: Madeira Street, Star Plaza, Golden Gates Shopping Center, and Nassau Street. (Anyone who was around at this time, could not have forgotten those mid-night sales). The partnership was dissolved in 1979.

The 1980's brought new investment opportunities. Wilcha Limited constructed a 38 unit-apartment/townhouse complex (Cable Beach Villas) on West Bay Street. In 1987 I partnered with my son and nephew in a company, McDel Ltd, for the development of the subdivision called Bahamia West. Both investments were completed in the 1990's.

Working with Lene

Throughout all these business ventures my wife Lene had been working by my side, supporting me through it all. She assisted me in preparing bills from the time we first got married until the late 1970's. She was then employed by Commonwealth Textiles and took over responsibility for stock-control and purchasing patterns and notions. Additionally, she would assist with sales during lunchtime or whenever any of the staff was off. Lene did not believe in being idle. Even when her family duties did not permit her to technically work "outside of the home", she sold Avon products to her neighbors in Sea Breeze Estates.

After the dissolution of Commonwealth Textiles Ltd, in 1979, Lene went full time into business and started the Commonwealth Fashion Center on Montgomery Street, now Commonwealth Fabrics. She successfully operated her business until her death in 2011. I still report to work every day at the store.

Left Image: *Commonwealth Textiles Building, Madeira Street.* ***Center Image:*** *Commonwealth Fabrics, Golden Gates Store, Sister Ruth Delancey, centre, manageress.* ***Right Image:*** *Commonwealth Textiles raffle draw. Photo: Gavin McCartney, Tammy McCartney, Tonya McCartney holding up winning tickets*

Commonwealth Textiles Staff: L-R: Lucille Clare (Arnold's mother-in-law), Addie McCartney, Eileen McCartney, Craig Delancey, Dr. Charlene Wallace & other employees.

Inside Palmdale Fashion Mall: Home of New Commonwealth Fabric

Left Image: *Wilcha Ltd. Cable Beach Townhouses on Cable Beach.*
Right Image: *Bahamia West subdivision, West Bay Street*

7
Family Life

Al Finds Love

My Uncle Timothy and Aunt Cora were also Lene's uncle and aunt. However, the distinction must be made that biologically, Timothy was my uncle, and Cora was Lene's aunt. Having this common bond, it was inevitable that we would not only meet, but also become "associated."

Lene as a teenager

It was at East Street Gospel Chapel that we "associated," as we both attended Sunday School there. My cousins liked me for her. I was my uncle Timmy's favorite nephew. He said even my aunt liked me. I had to pass their house on my way home. So, conveniently, I would stop everyday for lunch. My aunt liked that, I guess it was a great compliment to her cooking. Lene did not stand a chance against my persistence and our cousins' constant match-making efforts.

Despite the road-blocks, I knew what I wanted, and wasted no time in pursuing it. But my passion had to be bridled as the culture and protocol of the day dictated that I had to court my beloved for two years before we could marry.

Lene

Eliza Eileen Culmer McCartney affectionately called 'Lene', was born in Savanah Sound on February 19, 1931, the seventh child of the late Arthur Wardell Culmer and the late Sarah Claretta Culmer (Nee Sands).

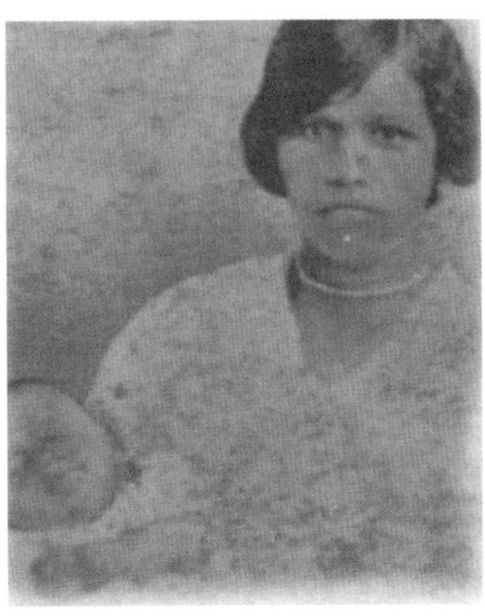

Al's Father-in-law, Arthur Culmer *Al's Mother-in-law, Sarah Culmer*

Lene attended the Savannah Sound All Age School in Eleuthera, and the family worshipped at Wesley Methodist Church. In 1942, when Lene was only 11 years old, tragedy struck, as her beloved mother died in childbirth. Her father re-married 6 months later, and soon after, Lene moved to

Hallandale, Florida, to help take care of the children of her older sister, Sarah 'Rita' Culmer Ingraham.

When she was 13 years old, Lene left Florida, bound for Savannah Sound. On the way to Eleuthera, however, her Uncle Timothy and Aunt Cora McCartney, who lived in Nassau, took her in to live with them and to assist them in cooking and taking care of the children. It was here Lene acquired and honed her famous culinary skills.

Al gets married at age 25

At the age of 25 years I married my lovely wife Eliza Eileen Culmer. Afterwards, it was full speed ahead for church and family. On Wednesday June 27th, 1951, I finished work at 3pm went upstairs, took a shower and dressed up in a white gabardine suit. I was collected by uncle George Ferguson in Taxi #35 and was driven to Zion Baptist Church where my best man and groomsmen were waiting.

At 5:00 pm my bride and I walked down the aisle of Zion Baptist Church on Shirley Street, and were joined in Holy Matrimony by Rev. Talmadge Sands (my wife's uncle). We had a full court of bridesmaids and groomsmen including Dr. Timothy McCartney, Robert Major, Will Bethel, Ivis McCartney-Carey, Cora Culmer-Sands, and Dorothy McCartney-Moncur. Clarice Sands-Granger was maid of honor and Archie Carey was best man. The Page boy was Philip Carey with Flower girls Cheryl Christie-Cash and Mavis McCartney. The organist was Mrs. Dora Sands (my wife's aunt and wife of Rev Tamalage Sands).

Wedding photo, Front row: Philip Carey (Ring Bearer), Cheryl Christie & Mavis McCartney (Flower Girls), Standing, L-R; Cora Culmer (sister of bride), Dorothy McCartney, Al, Lene, Clarice Sands, Rear: Timothy McCartney, Arthur Culmer, Cora McCartney, Archie Carey.

The bride & groom were driven by Mr. Lloyd Delancey (my brother-in-law) in his Buick. The bridesmaids were driven by Mr. George Ferguson (my uncle), best man was driven by Gladstone Christie (my uncle and father of Perry Christie) and relatives. We had no honeymoon as there was no money and no time. The next day was work.

The wedding reception was at Uncle Timmy's house as the hotels were off limits for colored people. I was very pleased that the reception was so well planned and executed. There was lots of food and wine. I figured that it was a lot of pressure on my aunt and uncle with us being their first niece and nephew. On our way home from the reception we stopped by my sister Ruth who had just given birth to Willie.

Al & Lene

Early Family Life

We moved to Mount Royal Avenue and Durham Street to begin the most exciting part of my journey in life. My wife, Eileen and I settled in our upstairs second story house overlooking a block of property from Clifton Street on the western side of Mount Royal Avenue. Auto repairs occurred on the ground-floor.

The house was semi-furnished with an apartment size gas stove financed by Bahamas Gas. The bed room suite was used and purchased on terms from F.A. Dean Furniture. My wife was a good cook and our first grocery supply was 1/2lb bologna sausage and rice.

My first order of business was to organize breakfast and later collect all the wedding gifts from Uncle Tim's House. As of today, September 2017, we still have most of our gifts in our china closet.

I wanted to set up my living quarters as comfortable as possible. My wife and I drove down to Uncle Tim's house collected our gifts and loaded them in the car that Granville Butler loaned me. He loaned me a car to use for a few days because I did not own a car. My wife and I brought in enough food for breakfast and lunch.

I was the first in the family to own and use a propane cooking gas range, a propane water heater, and a television. Children from the neighborhood would come upstairs on the porch and look through the windows to watch TV Reception from Florida that we got through a 40 foot high antenna on the roof. Reception was poor and 'snowy' most of the time.

My workshop on the lower floor also needed organizing. I set up my gas station pumps from Sinclair and products from Texaco. Mr. A.R. Braynen was the local agent for Sinclair Gas who agreed to install an underground tank and two pumps.

I hired some good mechanics and body repair men, like

Jamaican Keith Phillips, who was a good, neat body worker. Sam McQuay, and Everette Strachan who were also members of the Gospel Mission.

My wife, Lene, helped with bookkeeping and other records on finance and sales. I set up facilities for laundry that had one interesting feature. We hoisted our laundry up to the 2nd highest post.

George 'Spider' Rolle resided two properties west through Durham Street. He made friends with the family and later joined the company to learn bodywork. He learned quickly and stayed on for 10 years. He then relocated to his own body shop. George remained connected to my family, and is a good friend to this day. He also introduced me to the first property lot to purchase. I bought the lot and built a two story building that is still rented today.

The second purchase was a property adjoining my shop. The third property (two lots) on Mount Royal Avenue was purchased from my friend, Leroy Smith. Most young men and women in the neighborhood who came by were interested in learning the mechanical and body work trade. They were given an opportunity to do so.

There were no government regulations for minimum wage, labour laws, or compulsory insurance. So if a young person wanted to learn they were welcomed with no obligations to the company. By the third year after setting up our home and business I became very busy and had many customers.

Other businesses operating in the area at that time were Pinders Symphony Services on Montrose Avenue, that later became Bahamas Bus and Truck, operated by Mr. Frank Pinder; Nassau Repair shop on Mackey Street operated by Dennis Fountain; Brennen Brothers furniture making; Daniel Ferguson wood work shop on Madeira Street, and Malcolm's Service Station on Bay and Victoria Street. I began to make inquiries and to purchase surrounding properties as well as purchasing the entire block on the western side and half of the block on the eastern side.

After purchasing my 3rd property from Annette. A steel building was erected and used as storage for the tires and paint supplies. We then purchased a building across the street and built another steel building which was used for body repairs. As a result of the positive business integrity, McCartney's Auto Company Ltd. was then formulated and he company expanded into Freeport. My reasoning for selecting Freeport was a large Italian population employed at the casino and hotels. This provided an "easy sell" for the cars. The cars were imported from Italy and Japan and shipped to the two prime locations on Queen's Highway in Freeport and arranged for shipment to Nassau when needed, as mentioned earlier.

Used car lot Mt. Royal Avenue.

First Texaco Gas station dealership, Parts & auto repair shop, first residence upstairs

Lene and I were soon blessed with a son William (Billy) and the following year Barrett (Barry). We then we had Lennox (Lenny) and Keith McCartney. In 1965 we relocated to Sea Breeze Estate.

Al & Sons (Billy, Lenny, Keith, Barry

Family Photo at first family reunion, 1970, Sea Breeze house

Our life together was rich with shared memories. I remember that the first two boys, Billy and Barry were born within the first year of our marriage. They were born in the original homestead on Mount Royal Avenue and delivered by Nurse Naomi Christie (mother of Perry Christie).

During the labour and delivery of my first born, Billy, on July 7th 1952 at 11:00am, a problem occurred which caused concern to nurse Christie who was desperately attempting to get the 'afterbirth' (Placenta) delivered. She explained the situation, was worried, and wondered what to do. Lene was crying and in pain. I went downstairs and Dr. Roland Cumberbatch coincidentally drove up to my garage for service. I felt it was the Lord's direction. I informed him of our dilemma. He immediately picked up his doctor's bag, went upstairs, and in minutes the situation was cleared. What a relief!

Barry was a breach delivery and Lenny was the first to be born in the hospital. Because of my excitement, the Morris Minor I attempted to drive Lene to the hospital in broke down on Centerville Hill. Not that anything was wrong with the car. I think I was so excited that I just forgot how to operate it. I was so excited and nervous. A taxi had to take us to the hospital. By the time I went to pick up the car (it started right away), and when I got back to the hospital, Lenny was already born. Both Keith and Tammy, were born without incident.

As the boys developed, of course I wanted them to benefit from the same kind of Christian experience I had, but to take them to East Street Gospel Hall was too far. Fortunately, E. Jerome 'E.J.' Nottage began an outreach Ministry on Mt. Rose Avenue and Clifton St. It was called 'The Tabernacle'. His Ministry grew and developed quickly. He had lots of crusades and outreach. Soon, the youth classes and Sunday School were held. The Tabernacle showed The Billy Graham Films that ran for two weeks and was very crowded. Many were converted. We eventually moved back to East Street Gospel Hall.

In 1966, Tamara (Tammy) was born. Over the ensuing years, we as a couple had a few hard times, but there were lots of good times, for we truly believed that all things do work together for good to them that love the Lord.

Family vacations also provided sweet memories. My favourite family vacation was the one to Europe.

Family European trip 1969. West Berlin

The whole family was able to travel. We had 'caught ourselves' by then and had money. So, we bought round-trip, first-class tickets on British Airways to London.

Family European trip 1969. Tower of London

Family European trip 1969. East Berlin

After a week there we went to Paris. We didn't enjoy Paris because we couldn't speak French and it seemed that no-one there wanted to speak English. Our stay was only three days, then onto Berlin. We enjoyed Germany much more because we found an area that consisted mostly of Americans. Berlin was a memorable experience for me because I had been involved in the war effort back home, and so I got to see where Hitler's madness started. We also traveled to the Holy Land.

Holy Land Trip

TEXACO
TEXACO

DEALER
OF THE
MONTH
TRUST YOUR CAR
TO THE MAN
TEXACO

8
The Brethren Church

As a result of Queens College's decision not to accept Uncle Eris as a student, my grandfather, who was Methodist at the time, decided to join the Brethren Church. It was therefore natural for us to join Central Gospel Hall.

The Plymouth Brethren Movement

The Plymouth Brethren movement was believed to be an independent work of the Holy Spirit. The true church was established on the day of Pentecost. The two guiding principles were to be the breaking of bread every Lord's Day, and a ministry based upon the call of Christ rather than the ordination of men. They follow and obey the scripture, refusing to follow human tradition and creed. Others call them Brethren but they prefer to be called Christians.

In 1827, John Nelson Darby joined this group. Darby saw the church as a special work of God. Some years later Darby as an old man sat on a bench in Central Park, New York City. His clothing, which had been black, was not the best. His head was bare, bent forward, and his hat lay on his knees. A much younger man passing, thought him to be a beggar and dropped a dime in his hat. Darby looked up from his prayer and talked long and earnestly with the young man. That conversation led Charles Holder (the young man) to devote his life to the service of the Lord Jesus. After that incident the Brethren spread like wildfire through Spanish Wells and North Eleuthera.

A small Brethren faithful group remained on Harbour Island. In the 1930's on Dunmore Street, about 50 yards south of the Wesley Methodist Church, the Bible Truth Hall, under a Brethren preacher named Christopher Knapp operated until the 1980's when they closed due to the lack of members.

Van Ryn whose home was on Marsh Harbour described his 1926 visit to Cherokee Sound, Abaco.

"We would talk to anxious souls until late night and again early in the morning, along with the regular meetings. A number confessed the Lord. Toward the end of the two weeks, the fishing fleet came in. Long before the boat reached shore, the men aboard were waving their hats and shouting. Then we finally heard what they were saying. They were saying, "there's been a wonderful revival on our ships. Lots of men have been saved."

While the Lord moved hearts on their boats, unknown to them, he had saved children, wives, sweethearts, or parents back home. What rejoicing! About one hundred were saved in that little town. Soon they left for Spanish Wells. When those there heard about the awakening in Abaco, they said, "we hope we'll see something like that here". By eight o'clock that morning, 35 souls had been saved while alone in their own homes! The meetings continued and about one hundred more were saved.

Methodist Minister, F. Moon, reported the visit of an agent of Plymouth Brethren to Current, Spanish Wells and Harbour Island. Cecil Cartwright confirmed that it was Charles Holder, sometimes called 'the crazy preacher', after whom the sect gained the name of Holderites. From 1880, the

Holderites held services in private homes and by the Up Yonder Shipyard at Harbour Island until they were able to build their 'Halls'. Nassau merchant Thaddeus George Johnson built the first 'Bible Truth Hall' on Harbour Island and willed it to the Brethren on his death in 1921.

Of course, the Brethren were disliked by the Methodist Missionaries as they caused division in the church. George Lester remarked that "the Brethren were of the darkest description, as more had joined, and taken a wicked attitude toward the Church".

Cartwright told the story of the Spanish Wells man, who said of Holder: ***"I wish some hailstones would fall from the sky and split his bald head open."*** A few nights later some large hailstones did fall. Instead of on Holder, the hailstones fell on the head of the man who had wished him evil and injured him so severely that he died.

Evangelist W.H. Farrington

Growth of the Brethren Church

When the time was right to start East Street Gospel Hall, Brother W.H. Farrington located a property on East Street just north of McCollough Corner, adjacent to the Johnson's homestead. Brother Farrington discussed with the caretakers of this property who then contacted the owners that resided in the United States. The owner came and met The Brethren at Uncle Sonny McCartney's house on Lewis Street. Brother Farrington knew that there were families around to build a mission in this area. Men like Irvin McCartney's family whose wife was from the G.H. Thompson family, and the Lockhart family to name a few. They were spread throughout the expanding Mason's Addition. The Johnson family had good Christian workmen who were just what the Lord ordered. Farrington had taken a lease on this small lot of land adjacent to the Johnsons. They connected with Irvin McCartney and started a church there, initially in a tent.

The Johnsons and others soon built a small wooden church under a Mamey (fruit) tree. The Ministry expanded with a Sunday school that was held at 3:00 pm. The attendance grew to 400. Most of the young people from the surrounding areas (irregardless of their denomination) attended East Street Gospel Hall Sunday School at three o'clock every Sunday.

East Street Gospel Chapel　　*Blue Hill Gospel Chapel*

Freeport Gospel Chapel *Believer's Gospel Chapel*

Many Awards for Christian Service

Many young family members in the neighborhood attended East Street Gospel Hall. Many were converted - the Strachans from Culmersville and the Hannas from Mt. Royal Ave. Norma Hanna played the piano and joined the mission. Everette Strachan and family also joined. Many from other Brethren Assemblies came and helped some Sundays. Our Sunday School attendance increased. Over 200 became members as a result of Billy Graham films that were shown. Thousands attended and many responded to the Gospel and helped with Sunday School. I became one of the elders and helped to expand the Brethren Mission by assisting in establishing the Blue Hill Chapel, Freeport Gospel Chapel, Believers and "the premier" of our projects the Christian Life Centre (C.L.C.) It was there that I spent many full days on site. I also served as secretary to our associations and as president for terms lasting as long as 10 years. I visited and assisted with many of the projects.

Al, singing one of many solos

Christian Life Centre Groundbreaking

Al with Errol Jackson (standing), sitting: L-R; Cecil Cartwright, Al, Evangelist Tom Roberts, background: Marcel Lightbourne & Rex Major. Ladies seated: Wilma Curling, Olga McCartney, Lower R. Photo: Ned Wallace & Brother Perry Wallace, ground breaking: Herbert Johnson, Al, Cecil Cartwright, Errol Jackson. Background: Ned Wallace, Arnold McCartney

Al's Activities

I knew I loved the Lord. I truly wanted to be a part of converting others by demonstrating the Lord's work, by walking it and talking it, especially as I planned a family. So, I made my desire and commitment known. I chose a Sunday School evening after my grandfather preached a sermon on Revelation Chapter 3:20.

The invitation was given for anyone who was led, to accept the sacrifice of Christ Jesus, who sacrificed his life to save and redeem us. It was asked, "Would you now demonstrate it by standing", I stood up! I was then counseled, baptized and accepted as a member of the body of Christ and was ready to work to continue to tell and show others the way.

I then accepted many responsibilities of The Assemblies of Brethren. One of the first choir performances that went live on ZNS was led by me. They had to be fully dressed in the ZNS studio. This was prior to ZNS cameras recording outside of the studio.

Other church activities included:

- Teaching the bible class for many years
- Elected and served as elder Emeritus
- Secretary of the Association of Brethren
- Elder and secretary of our Elders
- President of The Association of Brethren
- Serving on the Christian Counsel
- Serving as president of The Christian Council
- Starting-up the Blue Hill Assembly
- Starting-up Believers Assembly
- Construction of Freeport Gospel chapel

- Helped to encourage the Gospel Proclamation Association members to place their assets in the Blue Hill Assembly
- Established the Cat Island Children's Home
- Assisting with the Christian Life Center Project
- Assisting with the Expansion of the East Street Assembly property

As I moved in and out of our Family's prayer sessions, through work and other commitments, I had no doubt that my name was often mentioned. I was always part of our Sunday School and taught Sunday School classes for many years. Church activities involved, solos in Sunday School and prize-giving. I vividly recall singing a song at Central Gospel Sunday School prize giving - #728 of the Redemption songs taught to me by my father. "My stubborn will at last hath yielded." Ms. Ruth Bethel, who later married Kendall Isaacs, played the piano. I felt it was performed very well and I believed it gave me the confidence to do better.

The traditional church picnic was held each August Monday holiday. Locations were initially at Montague and Yamacraw Beaches and eventually it moved to Adelaide and Love Beach as more space was needed.

Initially the Sunday Schools were held by Central Gospel and Bain Town Gospel. In later years as the Ministry expanded, East Street Gospel, Grace Gospel, and subsequently Blue Hill, and Engleston held Sunday Schools.

Evangelist W.H. Farrington had worked and built the Brethren Mission and The Brethren Ministry for many years on the family islands along with other, mostly foreign, missionaries.

Commitment to Accept Christ Age 24

At the age of 24, I made a commitment to accept Christ as my Lord and Saviour. I was then baptized and accepted into the fellowship of the assembly. As a member of East Street Gospel Chapel Sunday School and youth group, we organized the young people's fellowship in the early 1950's. Sunday evenings at 5:00pm was the radio program 'Youth Group'. We tried to perform efficiently as we were on the air and so we started and finished on time. At five o'clock the announcer would say, "This is youth time." The program would start promptly, and closing would be exactly at six o'clock.

Some weekends we would visit the park in Fox Hill, the Eastern Parade, and Montague Beach. Sometimes we would have meetings on the market range which would included boats from the family islands Cuba and Haiti.

Church Life

I always believed that once you put God first, all things will be added unto you. Ever since I accepted Christ as my personal savior at East Street Gospel Chapel age 18. I've been active in all aspects of the church. I've attended East Street Gospel Chapel from its inception, when services were held in a tent. I remain there to this day serving in the capacity of Elder, a position to which I was named in October 1969.

I was a part of the Men's Bible Class in the early 1950's. These classes were conducted by E.J. Nottage at The Tabernacle on Montrose Ave. I was also Master of Ceremony for the first radio broadcast from East Street Gospel Chapel in November 23rd, 1969.

I assisted with street meetings with the late W.H. Farrington when we held tent meetings. I also sang in the choir, with my sisters Ivis, Ruth, and Dot (the McCartney Quartet), and in a duet with my brother Arnold.

I was secretary and held other administrative positions in the church, namely, Sunday school teacher, choir director, preacher, elder (from October 1969), Cell Group leader and counselor. I served as President of the Assemblies of Brethren in The Bahamas, a position that I've held many times in the 80's through 2011.

Many projects have materialized under my watch including the birth of new churches namely, Blue Hill Gospel Chapel and Believers Gospel Chapel, and most recently the erection of the Christian Life Center on John F. Kennedy Drive.

I am loved, admired and highly respected not only among the Brethren Assemblies and the business community, but throughout the entire Commonwealth of The Bahamas. The Lord has blessed me through church, family and business life. Serving as Vice President and as President of the Association of Assemblies of Brethren (A.A.O.B) for some 15 years and remaining on the Committee of Management of the A.A.O.B. was an accomplishment. I presently serve on the building Committee, and recently, I was awarded Doctor of Divinity Degree in recognition of my ministerial and religious contributions.

Governor General Lady Marguerite Pindling placing CMG award medal,

On the 7th of January, 2016, Her Majesty the Queen Elizabeth II, acting on advice from the Governor General of the Commonwealth of The Bahamas, bestowed upon me the venerable award of Companion of the Most Distinguished order of Saint Michael and Saint George (C.M.G.).

Al, G-G Lady Marguerite Pindling, Prime Minister Perry Christie

R: Brother Arnold & wife Mary, Al, G-G Lady Marguerite Pindling, PM Perry Christie, sisters Angela Wallace & Dorothy Moncur, Brother-in-law Charles Wallace

The award was in recognition of my contributions to the Assemblies of the Brethren and for my entrepreneurial spirit. This was a very insightful award as it accurately depicts a summary of my life's mission on earth.

I have served on the oversight of my Assembly for about 50 years and I am one of the four surviving church members. I was also instrumental in the Gospel Rescue Mission. Ministering to the physical and spiritual needs of the young people in the 1950's.

I requested that the Pastoral Board relieve me of some of my Ministerial duties. My Ministerial portfolio was revised and allowed me devotion to full-fledged Pastoral duties. I continued my service to the Lord and church in the capacity as member of the finance and Cell Group Committees. I am also a representative for the church on the Committee of Management of the A.A.O.B in The Bahamas.

Bahamas Gospel Mission

After my first three sons were born I found myself working morning, noon and night. No one from East Street Gospel checked on my family.

T.B. Nottage, whenever he visited would walk from Madeira Street where he lived with his nephew, Jerome Nottage and would even go upstairs to visit with Lene.

Jerome E.J. Nottage invited me to come over to the mission. I gladly accepted. I worked alongside Sir Baltron Bethel who later married Helen, Jerome's daughter. Their wedding was held at the Tabernacle. I was the soloist and sang 'Wedding Prayer', by J. Smith of the People's Church in Toronto. It was ordered especially for the wedding.

Rescue Mission Moves to Montrose Avenue

One day Jerome (E.J.) Nottage paid me a visit and invited me to join and play a major role in Bahamas Gospel Mission.

I happily joined as the Mission was located just a block away from my residence. My oldest son, Billy, was 1 year old, and I wished to bring him under the influence of the church. I assisted with the mission, some of my staff also joined. Everette Strachan was also a big asset in the music sector as he quickly learned to blow the trumpet and he lived just two blocks away. Gweneth Munnings was also helpful. Sir Baltron Bethel also came over from Central Gospel and soon married Helen who played the piano. Norma Hanna also played an active role in the music department.

The most outstanding event was the Billy Graham Crusade films. A Billy Graham team came in for 2 weeks. Every night a one hour long gospel film of Billy Graham's Ministry was played to full capacity crowds numbering in the thousands. Brother Carter came from Florida with his team. Many people were converted and accepted Christ as their saviour and also joined other churches. One person who comes to mind was Brother Herbert Treco. He accepted Christ, joined Grace Community Church and became a leading Elder. He assisted in the development of Grace Community Ministry until his call to heaven. Many other persons accepted Christ at that two week crusade.

The Bahamas Gospel Rescue Mission outreach was focused on the youth. A bus drove to the function of Mackey & Shirley Street to collect dozens of young people and bring them back to the mission on Montrose Ave. Refreshments consisting of ham sandwiches and drinks were given to the youth before they left to go back. After spending approximately three years at the mission I decided to return to East Street where I continued the mission of discipleship. I continued to reach out to young boys in Sunday School as a teacher. I felt the need to collect preteen boys of our family and the surrounding neighborhoods and take them to Sunday School. Many benefited from that effort and some are serving in the church today.

Al's Involvement in the Vision for East Street Gospel Assembly

I am very proud of our church Sunday School. It has produced professionals, deacons, elders and it has been my privilege to be a part of its growth at the East Street Gospel Assembly. As our leadership grew and developed, we had to expand to other locations. Our first expansion was in the Blue Hill area where five of our elders and six deacons and their families resided. They were asked to relocate to the newly formed Blue Hill Gospel Chapel. Meanwhile, two elders were assigned to oversee Engleston Gospel Chapel as a vacancy was created by the passing of Evangelistic Addington Taylor.

Freeport needed a Ministry and our evangelist Hartley

Thompson filled that need and relocated to Freeport. Nassau assemblies supplied the necessary funds to erect the Freeport Gospel Assembly that now expanded to include an education facility that has over 300 students in attendance.

After approximately 15-20 years and after the East Street Assembly had developed another cadre of deacons and elders our members who resided in East New Providence were clamoring for expansion in the area of East New Providence. I truly believe the Lord planned for East Street Gospel Chapel. Soon one of our East Street members Mrs. Vylma Thompson-Curling, permanent secretary discovered that The Bahamas government was selling property on the Prince Charles Highway.

In church foyer with Sis. Vylma Curling & Bro. Barton Duncanson.

A lot in that area was available and it was purchased. Elder Ned Wallace drew the architectural plans and it was approved. Ned Wallace began to build. After almost reaching the rebar, God called Ned Home to glory and the building stalled. At this juncture East Street Chapel was completely out of funds and the site became overgrown with monkey tamarind as high as the rebar.

Freeport Gospel Chapel Assembly

Evangelist Hartley Thompson of the East Street Gospel heard the call to go into Grand Bahama where he joined the group headed by Theophilus who held services in his home in Freeport. Brother Hartley joined him until Brother Theophilus decided to relocate and allow the church to operate from the dwelling. Application was then made by the association to the Grand Bahama Port Authority requesting the option to lease land and build a chapel. The request was granted, and the Nassau Brethren borrowed from R.B.C $100,000.00 to construct and complete the chapel.

Photo with best friend & brother-in-law Archie Carey

Believers Gospel Chapel

One day, Archie Carey who lived in the area, passed and observed the state of the Believers Gospel Chapel. Archie Carey and I went into our personal savings account and accumulated enough money from our savings to complete the church building to its rebar. East Street Chapel Assembly was requested to credit enough material from Kelly's Lumber to complete the roof and continue the building until the chapel was good enough to occupy. All members who resided in east New Providence were asked to relocate. I did not relocate as I felt the call of God to remain at East Street Chapel as the Christian Life Center was on the drawing board. The cost for erecting this facility was $10 million.

Christian Life Center

The assemblies have always prayed for a facility that could house and be the headquarters of the many ministries and house the College of The Brethren. It was the hand of God acting when Brother Cecil Cartwright came across 11.5 acres of property on J.F.K Drive. He immediately came to me to accompany him to walk the boundary. We then made an offer to Christie's Real Estate. The offer of $175,000 was accepted and the deal was presented to the assembly in Nassau. The assembly accepted and each assembly made their contributions. Central Gospel, East Street Assembly, Grace Community, Blue Hill Assembly, and Emmanuel Gospel Assembly each gave $35,000.

The money was paid and the United Assemblies took possession. Architectural plans were drawn and approved by the Ministry of Works. Unfortunately, attempts were made to access the property but were hampered by the Higgs family, sometimes armed with shotguns. Eventually, the Higgs family discontinued their claim and the assemblies were able to build.

Ceremony naming Christian Life Centre entrance in his honor

I was appointed president of the Association of Brethren and assisted in construction of the Christian Life Center, the Blue Hill Assembly, Freeport Gospel Chapel, Believers Gospel Chapel, and East Street Gospel Chapel expansion. I received many awards for Christian service and leadership from Mount Tabor Church, East

Street Gospel Assembly, and from Dr. Philip Rahming. I was made a Brethren Hero, C.L.C president (Christ Community Church), along with previously receiving the most distinguished order of St. Michael and St. George (C.M.G.). Presented by Lady Pindling from Her Majesty Queen Elizabeth II.

Photo with Bro. James Shearer

Al & Lene flanked by daughter Tammy & son Lennox

Award ceremony for Doctor of Divinity (wife Eileen behind)

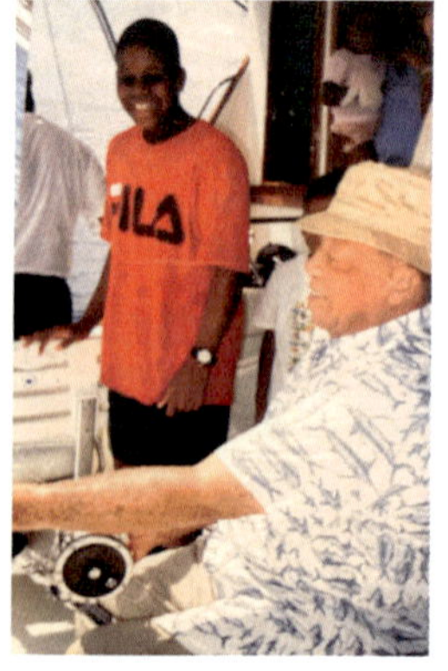

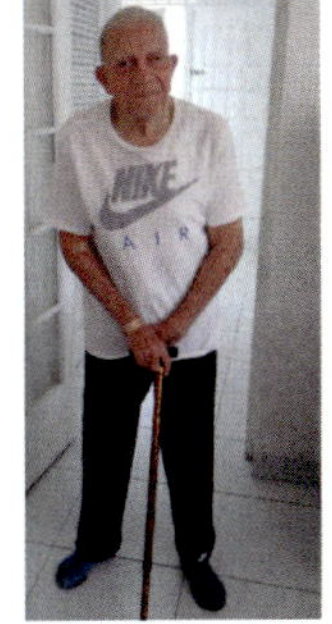
NIKE
AIR

45

9
A Very Anxious Time

Father, Alfred Arnold McCartney

About my Father

My father, Alfred Arnold McCartney, who was born Nov 7, 1898 became mentally ill for a period. He had to be admitted to the Bahamas General Hospital (now Princess Margaret Hospital), and placed in security for a period. His 'nervous' condition was caused, we believe, by pressure of family economic needs. I recall at the time he was employed as a cashier for a grocery establishment on Bay Street (near the market range) at a salary of 10 shillings per week.

Suddenly he stood up, not speaking or responding to questions. He was taken home in a surrey and later taken to the hospital where he was detained and admitted to the 'crazy hall' section of the hospital for two weeks.

He was sometimes in a room with iron bars. This was heart-breaking for me. I would visit him daily. On one occasion while sitting on a bench on the outside of his room, he shouted, "Al do not hop on that truck!" He would hurt his arm trying to force it between the bars.

Meanwhile, my mother was able to secure employment at Bahamas General Hospital in the kitchen of the nurse's residence. I vividly remember her employment because, on my way to Sunday School at Central Gospel Hall, I would pass by and would be handed a cup of jello. Wow, I can taste it now!

In 1966 my father was admitted to the Rassin Hospital because of liver cancer and I eventually received permission from Dr. Meyer Rassin for Billy and I to take him to Miami to seek a second opinion. Dr. Rassin had indicated to my sister, Dot (who was a R.N. on his staff) that he did not expect him to survive as there was nothing more medicine had to offer. Before we left for Miami L.B. Johnson interviewed my father and encouraged my father to reveal his wishes for any real estate owned by him so it could be documented in case he passes away. On June 5, 1966 my father told him "that he had already given instructions to Al and he had no doubt that it will be carried out according to his wishes". A lot of land was given to his four daughters, lots #5 and #6 was given to Arnold and I to be used at our discretion.

Each daughter built a small house on their lot. Arnold and I built a two-story building which housed the auto repair shop and used car parts on the ground floor and there were two, two bedroom apartments on the second floor. These apartments and the garage were able to support my father after he retired. The other property was shared between Al and Arnold with one lot going to East Street Gospel Chapel.

His one tenth share in Eleuthera properties would automatically rest with Al who was under advice. The property was distributed as my father directed. After three days in Jackson Memorial Hospital my mother who stayed to take care of him called to say my father had gotten worse and, although I planned to go over to Miami the next day, my father informed my mother that he felt that I would be too late.

My Father passed away and my mother returned to Nassau. Butler's Funeral Home arranged with a Miami undertaker to have his body flown back to Nassau. The Mayor of Miami (Faircloth) was instrumental in having the expenses covered for repatriation. The funeral service was held at the East Street Gospel Chapel, burial at Ebenezer's Cemetery.

10
Conclusion

My life has been marked with great sacrifice and devotion to duty. The result has been great achievements and accomplishments.

Proverbs 3:5-6 “Trust in the Lord with all thy heart; and lean not unto thine own understanding. In all thy ways acknowledge him, and he shall direct thy path.”

Made in the USA
Middletown, DE
24 February 2024

50279746R00051